Color Me
FARTS

Color Me Farts

13-Digit ISBN: 978-1-64643-351-3
10-Digit ISBN: 1-64643-351-3

This book may be ordered by mail from the publisher. Please include $5.99 for postage and handling. Please support your local bookseller first!

Books published by Cider Mill Press Book Publishers are available at special discounts for bulk purchases in the United States by corporations, institutions, and other organizations. For more information, please contact the publisher.

Cider Mill Press Book Publishers
"Where Good Books Are Ready for Press"
501 Nelson Place
Nashville, Tennessee 37214

cidermillpress.com

Typography: Epicursive Script, Filson Pro

Printed in the United States of America

23 24 25 26 27 VER 7 6 5 4 3

Color Me FARTS

A Hilarious Adult Coloring Book

CIDER MILL PRESS

BOOK PUBLISHERS

Introduction

Tooting, breaking wind, cutting the cheese—no matter how much we might want to deny it, we all fart. Some farts are louder than others, some call more attention to themselves by how they smell, but all farts are the same in that they are the result of a healthy body releasing gas built up from the foods we eat and the air we breathe. And although not everyone might want to admit it, many of us have been in the presence of a friend or loved one passing gas and found it endearing, or downright cute.

As certain as the fact that we all fart, it is unquestionable that people of all ages will find this adorably funny coloring book outrageously cute. Do all animals fart? No. But most of them do and even for those that don't, like birds, seeing images of them in their natural habitats releasing an air biscuit will bring a smile to your face.

The same as all of our farts are different, the pages that follow can be made wholly distinctive based on your mood and tastes. Beyond the quirky appeal of these illustrations is the ability to make them your own, and in doing so tune out the rest of the world for a while and enjoy the alone time . . . free to color and fart as much as you like.

Don't be shy about something
that is completely natural! Share your
colorful creations with the world by
posting on social media with the
hashtag #colormefarts (and be
sure to tag us @cidermillpress).
Now go forth and color!

Share Your
MASTERPIECES

Don't keep your colorful creations to yourself—take a pic and share it on social media with the hashtag **#colormefarts** and tag us @cidermillpress!

#COLORMEFARTS #COLORMEFARTS
#COLORMEFARTS #COLORMEFARTS
#COLORMEFARTS #COLORMEFARTS
#COLORMEFARTS #COLORMEFARTS
#COLORMEFARTS #COLORMEFARTS
#COLORMEFARTS #COLORMEFARTS
#COLORMEFARTS #COLORMEFARTS
#COLORMEFARTS #COLORMEFARTS
#COLORMEFARTS #COLORMEFARTS
#COLORMEFARTS #COLORMEFARTS
#COLORMEFARTS #COLORMEFARTS
#COLORMEFARTS #COLORMEFARTS
#COLORMEFARTS #COLORMEFARTS
#COLORMEFARTS #COLORMEFARTS
#COLORMEFARTS #COLORMEFARTS
#COLORMEFARTS #COLORMEFARTS
#COLORMEFARTS #COLORMEFARTS
#COLORMEFARTS #COLORMEFARTS
#COLORMEFARTS #COLORMEFARTS
#COLORMEFARTS #COLORMEFARTS

#COLORMEFARTS #COLORMEFARTS
#COLORMEFARTS #COLORMEFARTS
#COLORMEFARTS #COLORMEFARTS
#COLORMEFARTS #COLORMEFARTS
#COLORMEFARTS #COLORMEFARTS
#COLORMEFARTS #COLORMEFARTS
#COLORMEFARTS #COLORMEFARTS
#COLORMEFARTS #COLORMEFARTS
#COLORMEFARTS #COLORMEFARTS
#COLORMEFARTS #COLORMEFARTS
#COLORMEFARTS #COLORMEFARTS
#COLORMEFARTS #COLORMEFARTS
#COLORMEFARTS #COLORMEFARTS
#COLORMEFARTS #COLORMEFARTS
#COLORMEFARTS #COLORMEFARTS
#COLORMEFARTS #COLORMEFARTS
#COLORMEFARTS #COLORMEFARTS
#COLORMEFARTS #COLORMEFARTS
#COLORMEFARTS #COLORMEFARTS
#COLORMEFARTS #COLORMEFARTS

#COLORMEFARTS #COLORMEFARTS
#COLORMEFARTS #COLORMEFARTS
#COLORMEFARTS #COLORMEFARTS
#COLORMEFARTS #COLORMEFARTS
#COLORMEFARTS #COLORMEFARTS
#COLORMEFARTS #COLORMEFARTS
#COLORMEFARTS #COLORMEFARTS
#COLORMEFARTS #COLORMEFARTS
#COLORMEFARTS #COLORMEFARTS
#COLORMEFARTS #COLORMEFARTS
#COLORMEFARTS #COLORMEFARTS
#COLORMEFARTS #COLORMEFARTS
#COLORMEFARTS #COLORMEFARTS
#COLORMEFARTS #COLORMEFARTS
#COLORMEFARTS #COLORMEFARTS
#COLORMEFARTS #COLORMEFARTS
#COLORMEFARTS #COLORMEFARTS
#COLORMEFARTS #COLORMEFARTS
#COLORMEFARTS #COLORMEFARTS

#COLORMEFARTS #COLORMEFARTS
#COLORMEFARTS #COLORMEFARTS
#COLORMEFARTS #COLORMEFARTS
#COLORMEFARTS #COLORMEFARTS
#COLORMEFARTS #COLORMEFARTS
#COLORMEFARTS #COLORMEFARTS
#COLORMEFARTS #COLORMEFARTS
#COLORMEFARTS #COLORMEFARTS
#COLORMEFARTS #COLORMEFARTS
#COLORMEFARTS #COLORMEFARTS
#COLORMEFARTS #COLORMEFARTS
#COLORMEFARTS #COLORMEFARTS
#COLORMEFARTS #COLORMEFARTS
#COLORMEFARTS #COLORMEFARTS
#COLORMEFARTS #COLORMEFARTS
#COLORMEFARTS #COLORMEFARTS
#COLORMEFARTS #COLORMEFARTS
#COLORMEFARTS #COLORMEFARTS
#COLORMEFARTS #COLORMEFARTS

About
CIDER MILL PRESS
BOOK PUBLISHERS

Good ideas ripen with time. From seed to harvest,
Cider Mill Press brings fine reading, information, and
entertainment together between the covers of its creatively
crafted books. Our Cider Mill bears fruit twice a year,
publishing a new crop of titles each spring and fall.

"Where Good Books Are Ready for Press"

501 Nelson Place
Nashville, Tennessee 37214

cidermillpress.com